MARCO MADE EASY

★ ★ ★

This book is dedicated to Mirabelle,
the most beautiful girl in the world

MARCO MADE EASY

A Three-Star Chef Makes It Simple

MARCO PIERRE WHITE

WEIDENFELD & NICOLSON

BEFORE you reach for the chopping board…

I've got a pub in Berkshire and like to head there when life in London becomes chaotic. Actually, the Yew Tree – with its Inglenook fireplace and cosy, warm dining room – is my favourite place in the world, though after a drop of Old Rosie cider you need to watch out for the low-beamed ceiling.

I was there the other night when a man came up to me and asked if I'd buy him a drink. 'Sir,' I said, 'the only thing on the house is the roof.' He laughed so, of course, I pulled him a pint.

And I was at the Yew Tree when I was presented with a dish that inspired this book. It was steak tartare, that dish of minced raw beef. As I stared at the plate it struck me that except for the steak and the raw egg yolk on top of it, most of the other ingredients came straight out of bottles. Tomato ketchup, mayonnaise, mustard, Worcestershire sauce and Tabasco – they all bring flavour to the dish and they are probably in your store-cupboard.

As I ate, I thought it might be a good idea to do a cookery book in which the main ingredient is not messed around with, but rather celebrated and shown off.

Too often cookery books try too hard and therefore they make the reader try too hard. I just don't get it. Life is complicated enough without introducing stress into the kitchen.

I like to keep things simple, and this book is all about creating beautiful and delicious food without any aggro. It's about producing big flavours, and the beauty of it all is that more often than not, no kitchen skill is required. You don't, for instance, need to be an artist to fold sea bass in tin foil. Equally,

the moules marinière and the peppered steak are two dishes that, when done well, will win smiles at any table in the land, but will not make the cook sweat.

This book is for anyone who loves food. The accomplished gourmet will appreciate the desire to show off the primary ingredient of a dish. The aspiring beginner or infrequent cook, on the other hand, can take comfort that most of the recipes need little know-how and little time.

In fact, it will take you longer to wash the dishes than it will to cook them.

The most commonly used phrase within these pages is 'to your taste'. In other words, taste, taste and taste – food that is perfect for you and your tastebuds.

Regularly I come across people who say they are frightened of cooking – they think they will mess it up, make a mistake. It is not just the aspiring home cook who suffers a fear of the stove. I've seen it in professional kitchens; those moments when a chef is petrified of taking centre stage at the hob. I really hope that these pages will instill confidence and dissolve the fear of the stove.

In *White Heat*, my first cookery book (it was published in 1990), I wrote, 'I can't work in a domestic kitchen; it's just too confined. There's no freedom and there's no buzz. At home I'm not hit with forty covers in half an hour so there's no real excitement.'

I've had to reassess my views after retiring from the professional kitchen more than a decade ago. Whether at home or in a restaurant, cooking has always been a way of life for me (I fell in love with it because it was the only way in which I could express myself). Cooking for guests in a restaurant is a tough job: the days are long and the nights are short. However, cooking for family and friends at home can't work if it is not a pleasurable experience. It has to be fun, and I hope that the ease of the recipes in this book will make you want to spend more time in the kitchen creating lovely meals. At home these days I am not hit with forty covers, but there is certainly a buzz to be had from making meals and I have long since discovered the freedom of my kitchen at home. (I have discovered the joys of shopping, too. I have to say, I love a shelf, I love a bottle and I love an aisle. That's why I got married three times.)

And on the subject of freedom, please use my recipes as a guide only. Don't feel restricted. Add or delete ingredients, as you see fit. Amend measurements, quantities and cooking times to suit your palate and your oven.

I declare an interest or two – I work with Knorr and within these pages I use Knorr's A Touch of Taste and their stock cubes. I use them because they add flavour and I treat them as a seasoning. If you disapprove don't use them. Likewise, I work with Bernard Matthews and in this book you will find turkey recipes. I love turkey and when cooked well – rather than dry – it is superior to most poultry.

I come from a background of training in classical French cuisine. As I worked my way up the ladder in the '70s and early '80s I was privileged to be mentored by the some of the greats, and it follows that many of the dishes that I have made over the years have been complex and required exceptional skill and knowledge in cooking techniques.

Here, I have used that skill, knowledge and experience to come up with recipes that are fool-proof – but I have also tried to provide recipes for that dish which will create a sense of occasion that is vital for the Saturday night dinner party or Sunday lunch gathering. Also, each dish is photographed so that, if you like, you can copy my presentation.

But remember when cooking that all great chefs have three things in common. First, they accept and respect that Mother Nature is the true artist and that they are the cook. Second, everything they do is an extension of themselves. And third, they give you insight into the world they were born into, the world that inspired them, and they serve it on their plates.

A few minor points… When recipes refer to olive oil that'll be extra virgin olive oil; I also use clarified butter (or ghee) because I like it, but by all means use your favourite butter or an oil if you prefer. Salted or unsalted butter? Always unsalted then you can add salt to your taste. When I refer to 'garnish' I am not thinking merely of decoration but also of ingredients that can be eaten, and be generous with it. When I talk of shrimps in the Shellfish section it is because I hate the word 'prawns'. The Americans say 'shrimp' and I quite like that. When using a fan-assisted oven, decrease the temperature and cooking time accordingly.

A final rule - rebellious members of the family (young and old) must flick through these pages: gastronomy, you see, is the greatest therapy to which any misfit can be exposed. And I should know.

I hope this little cookbook brings as much enjoyment to the person who is doing the cooking as it surely will to the person who is doing the eating. Me? I'm off to lunch at Wheeler's of St James's…

You're going to see a lot of herbs in this book. Why? Because they are fresh, vibrant, add colour and create flavour. The avocado with fresh herbs was inspired by a trip to Jamaica. Avocados are gigantic in Jamaica, and their shape resembles the island's green hills. There are lots of easy starters here too. The smoked salmon is presented just the way it was when I was a teenager and worked in the kitchen at The Box Tree. But simplicity is the key – nothing in this chapter is too complicated.

Starters

★ ★ ★

Avocado with fresh crab and herbs

Serves 1

About 50g white crab meat
Lemon juice
Maldon salt
Extra virgin olive oil
1 avocado
Fresh herbs of your choice,
   to garnish

1 Season the crab meat to your taste with a drop or three of lemon juice, a little salt and olive oil.
2 Carefully peel the avocado and slice it in half horizontally, so that you end up with a top and a bottom. Remove the stone and slice away the base so that the avocado bottom is flat underneath and can stand up on a plate.
3 Fill the centre of the avocado with crab meat and put the top half of the avocado on the crab meat.
4 Using a pastry brush, paint olive oil on to the avocado and onto the herbs. Stick the herbs on to the side – the oil should hold them.

Smoked salmon

Serves 1

1 Wallpaper a plate with a single layer of smoked salmon. Use kitchen scissors to remove the overlap by cutting around the rim of the plate. Eat the overlapping salmon – that's the cook's treat.
2 Serve with the lemon in the centre of the plate, ready to be squeezed over the fish.

About 180g good quality
   smoked salmon
½ lemon, wrapped in muslin

Carpaccio of yellowfin tuna à la Niçoise

Serves 2

About 30g tapenade
Extra virgin olive oil
20g red peppers from a
    jar, drained and diced
½ courgette, finely sliced
    and diced
2 slices of very fresh tuna,
    about 80g each
Fresh basil and coriander
    (or fresh herbs of your
    choice), to garnish
1 lemon

1 Mix the tapenade with a tablespoon of olive oil and set aside. Pour a tablespoon of olive oil over the red peppers and set aside.
2 Blanch the courgette by putting it into a saucepan of boiling water for 20 seconds. Quickly refresh the courgette by draining it in a colander and immediately running it under cold water for a few seconds. Set aside.
3 Flatten the tuna slices by putting the fish in the middle of a large chopping board and covering with a layer of clingfilm. Using the base of a saucepan (or, if you have one, a meat hammer), bash the tuna to flatten it. Ideally, the bashing should increase the surface area of the tuna by two or three times, so that it's about the depth of a £1 coin.
4 Carefully use the clingfilm to transfer the fish to a plate, then peel it away. Pour a teaspoon of olive oil onto the tuna and, using your fingers or a pastry brush, rub or brush it into the fish so that the surface glistens.
5 Spread the tapenade across the tuna and scatter over the diced pepper, diced courgette and basil or coriander. Add a dash of the olive oil and give the lemon a squeeze or two over the fish.

By the way… Tapenade is very salty so be sure to taste the dish before seasoning with salt.

14

Gravlax with mustard dressing

Serves 1

300ml water
200ml vinegar
100g sugar
¼ cucumber, peeled,
    deseeded and finely sliced
About 180g gravlax salmon
Baby fennel leaves (or fresh
    herbs of your choice),
    to garnish

For the mustard dressing
4 egg yolks
½ litre vegetable oil
4 heaped tablespoons
    Dijon mustard
4 tablespoons white
    wine vinegar
2 tablespoons caster
    sugar
Maldon sea salt

1 In a saucepan bring to the boil the water, vinegar and sugar, and then remove the pan from the heat. Leave to cool down for a minute or two before pouring the mixture over the sliced cucumber.
2 Make the dressing by whisking together all of the mustard dressing ingredients.
3 Wallpaper the plate with the gravlax and use kitchen scissors to trim around the rim of the plate. Eat the trimmings.
4 Arrange the cucumber slices on top of each other in the middle of the gravlax and scatter the baby fennel leaves on and around the cucumber.
5 Dress the gravlax with the mustard dressing.

Steak tartare Americaine

Serves 4

3 tablespoons tomato ketchup
20 drops Tabasco
4 teaspoons Hellmann's
  mayonnaise
4 tablespoons Worcestershire
  sauce
1 teaspoon mustard
2 teaspoons mashed
  anchovies
4 teaspoons chopped
  cornichons
4 teaspoons finely chopped
  shallots
4 teaspoons capers
450g rump steak, trimmed
  and minced (ask the butcher
  to do this for you)
4 eggs
Black pepper
Maldon sea salt
Fresh flat-leaf parsley
  (or fresh herbs of your
  choice), to garnish

1 Add all the ingredients, except the eggs, seasoning and parsley, to the minced steak and mix thoroughly.
2 Divide into four and make nice neat shapes. Make a little dip with a spoon in the top of each one. Crack the eggs, separate them, and put each yolk in a half shell on top of each portion of beef.
3 Add a twist of black pepper, a pinch of sea salt and a little parsley, to serve.

Salad of boiled ham and mushrooms with parsley

Serves 1

80g good quality ham
A handful of closed cup
  mushrooms
Sherry vinegar, to your taste
Extra virgin olive oil, to
  your taste
Fresh flat-leaf parsley
  (or herbs of your choice),
  to garnish

1 Finely slice the ham into strips the size of matchsticks. Finely slice the mushrooms to the same size.
2 Bring the ham and mushrooms together in a bowl and gently mix together with your fingertips. Drizzle over the sherry vinegar and olive oil and mix with your fingertips. Scatter parsley over the plate before eating.

Salade Lyonnaise

Serves 1

1 In a non-stick frying pan, fry the diced bacon until perfect for you.

2 Don't bother about making a vinaigrette dressing, just splash the frisée leaves with olive oil and then white wine vinegar. Using your hands, toss the salad so that the oil and vinegar coat the leaves. Now poach the egg.

3 In a bowl, assemble the salad like this: frisée, croûtons, perch the poached egg on top of the croûtons, then sprinkle over the bacon and the parsley or chervil. Top with a splash of olive oil, a pinch of sea salt, and finally, flick half a pinch of black pepper onto the white of the egg.

1 rasher good quality streaky bacon, diced
Extra virgin olive oil, for frying and dressing
½ frisée salad (also known as curly endive), heart only
White wine vinegar
1 egg
Croûtons
Fresh parsley or chervil (or fresh herbs of your choice), to garnish
Maldon sea salt and cracked black pepper

Beetroot and goat's cheese salad with walnuts

Serves 2

1 large (or 2 medium-sized) cooked beetroot
1 teaspoon Merlot vinegar
1 teaspoon extra virgin olive oil
40g-60g goat's cheese, broken into large crumbs
1 walnut, chopped into small pieces
Fresh herbs of your choice, to garnish

1 Finely slice the beetroot into circles and arrange the slices on a plate so that they slightly overlap each other.

2 Pour the teaspoon of vinegar onto the beetroot, in the centre of the plate. Using your fingertips or a pastry brush, spread it over the beetroot. Now pour the teaspoon of olive oil into the centre of the plate and again, using your fingertips or a pastry brush, spread it over the beetroot – it will add flavour and make the beet glisten. Scatter over the goat's cheese, chopped walnut and fresh herbs.

By the way…Ideally, a mandolin will slice the beetroot to the perfect width. The beetroot can be sliced, clingfilmed and stored in the fridge ahead of making the salad. If you don't have Merlot to hand, use a vinegar that you like.

Devils on horseback

Serves 10–20

Tabasco sauce, to your taste
200g mango chutney
20 rashers good-quality
    streaky bacon
20 Agen prunes, stoned

1 Preheat the grill. Add 5–10 drops of Tabasco to the mango chutney and taste it, adding more Tabasco if required.

2 Lay out the bacon rashers on a board. Spoon a dollop of the chutney mixture onto each rasher and put a prune on top. Roll up tight and cook them under the grill, turning once or twice, until the bacon has caramelised to your taste.

Pear and endive salad with Gorgonzola and walnuts

Serves 2

1 Finely slice the endive lengthways. Slice the pear lengthways into quarters and then slice each quarter into matchsticks. Cut the walnut into a dozen or so little pieces.

2 Put the pear matchsticks and sliced endive into a mixing bowl and pour over the walnut oil, followed by the sherry vinegar. Sprinkle with a pinch of sea salt. Use your fingers to mix gently, so that the pear and endive are coated in the flavours of the walnut oil and sherry vinegar.

3 Now simply build up the salad on the plates: first, endive, then cubes of Gorgonzola, then scatter over the chopped walnut, a little more endive, followed by more Gorgonzola… and continue to build. Finish by scattering over the parsley.

1 endive
1 pear
1 walnut, chopped into
   small pieces
1 dessertspoon walnut oil
1 teaspoon sherry vinegar
   (or vinegar of your choice)
Maldon sea salt
80g Gorgonzola cheese,
   cut into cubes
Fresh flat-leaf parsley (or
   fresh herbs of your choice),
   to garnish

By the way… The sweetness of the pear contrasts with the bitterness of the cheese. Roquefort can be used instead of Gorgonzola, though I prefer the latter. Similarly, I like Comice pears, but use your favourite variety – though for this salad, make sure the fruit is perfectly ripe. When mixing a salad with your fingers gentlessness is crucial – the ingredients have done you no harm so why rough them up?

I don't like the word prawns. I much prefer shrimp, as the Americans say. In this chapter you'll find seven dishes devoted to what I call shrimp, and my particular favourite is shrimp with whisky and girolles – it's all about earthiness and the sea, and I think it works extremely well.

The trick is to cook them rapidly, thereby ensuring their flavour and succulence. Likewise, my recipe for moules marinière involves just a few minutes at the hob…and is made, unusually, with no cream.

Shellfish

★ ★ ★

Fresh Cornish crab with herbs

Serves 1

About 100g brown crab meat
Lea & Perrins Worcestershire
   sauce
Tabasco sauce
100g white crab meat
Maldon sea salt
Lemon juice
Extra virgin olive oil
Meat of 2 crab claws, diced
Crispy Sardinian bread,
   or a bread of your choice
Fresh herbs of your choice,
   to garnish

1 Season the brown crab meat with Worcestershire sauce and Tabasco to your taste. Season the white crab meat with salt, a squeeze of lemon and a splash of olive oil.

2 Arrange the white crab meat on the plate and put the empty claws around it. Spoon the brown crab meat onto the other side of the plate. Place the crispy Sardinian bread between the white and brown meat.

3 Dot the plate with the diced crab claw and drizzle the bread with olive oil. Dress the plate with fresh herbs – be it basil, fresh mint or parsley. Season with salt before serving.

Fresh Cornish crab with ginger, pink grapefruit and coriander

Serves 1

About 100g white crab meat
Maldon sea salt
Extra virgin olive oil
½ pink grapefruit
100g brown crab meat
A pinch of curry powder
Meat of 2 crab claws, sliced
1 small piece of fresh ginger,
  peeled and finely sliced
  into wafer-thin matchsticks
Crispy Sardinian bread,
  or bread of your choice
Fresh coriander leaves and
  chives (or fresh herbs of
  your choice), to garnish

1 Season the white crab meat to your taste with a pinch of salt then drizzle over the olive oil and a squeeze of pink grapefruit juice.
2 Arrange the white and brown crab meat on the plate, keeping the meat separate.
3 Peel the grapefruit and cut into segments and then dice each segment.
4 Sprinkle over the curry powder, as if it were a seasoning – again, it's to your taste. Garnish with the grapefruit, ginger, coriander and chives and dot the sliced crab claw around the plate. Put the Sardinian bread between the white and brown meat and flick a pinch of salt over the bread.

Moules marinière, classic

Serves 2

1kg live mussels
100g unsalted butter, softened
100ml extra virgin olive oil
100ml white wine
3 sprigs of fresh thyme and
    2 bay leaves (or fresh herbs
    of your choice), to garnish

1 Give yourself 5 minutes to clean the mussels like this… running them under cold water, remove any loose grit from the shells and pull away the green beards. You only want to cook the mussels that are alive. To find out if the mussels are dead or alive tap them gently; if the shells close they are alive. If the shells don't move, discard them, and toast your good health.

2 In a small mixing bowl, whisk the butter with the olive oil then set aside.

3 Heat a casserole or a large saucepan with a lid. Pour in the wine and let it boil for about 30 seconds. Now add the mussels and slam on the lid. Steam over a medium-high heat for 2, 3, or even 4 minutes until all the mussels have opened. Discard any mussels that are still closed and toast your good health again.

4 Remove the pan from the heat and stir in the butter mixture so that it coats the fish and the shells. Shake the pan to ensure the mussels are buttery.

5 Add the thyme and bay leaves. Replace the lid and give the pan another good shake to spread the flavours and bouquet of the herbs. Serve immediately.

We all know fish and lemon works.
But what about fish and orange?
Halibut and orange: two ingredients.
Bring them together and you're
looking at the perfect summer lunch,
but have you ever heard of a simpler
dish to make?

You can't mess up these fish dishes
and the sea bass en papillote – once
tried and it will become a favourite
in your home.

Fish

★ ★ ★

Yellowfin tuna steak, Oriental-style

Serves 2

1 teaspoon dark soy sauce
Extra virgin olive oil, for
   dressing and brushing
1 teaspoon toasted sesame oil
1 piece fresh ginger, peeled
   and cut lengthways into
   matchsticks
Spring onions, sliced
   lengthways
2 tuna steaks, about 180g each
Maldon sea salt
Fresh herbs of your choice,
   to garnish

1 Make a dressing by combining the soy sauce,
a teaspoon of olive oil and sesame oil.
2 Blanch the ginger matchsticks by putting them
into a saucepan of boiling water for 20 seconds.
As soon as the water boils, drain the ginger, pouring
the hot water momentarily over the spring onions,
just enough to soften them. Refresh the ginger by
holding it under cold water for a few seconds. Pour
the dressing over the ginger and spring onions
and set aside.
3 Rub each side of the tuna steaks with olive oil or
brush with a pastry brush. Season the fish with half
a pinch of salt just before it goes into the dry pan.
Fry for about 90 seconds on each side, or longer
depending on the thickness of the steaks.
4 Serve with the ginger and spring onions on top
and around the tuna steaks.

A whole sea bass roasted for about 12 minutes and garnished with wild mushrooms

Serves 2

4 tablespoons extra virgin
    olive oil
1 whole sea bass, about 1kg
150g wild mushrooms
Clarified butter
Fresh parsley, finely chopped

1 Preheat the oven to 190°C/gas 5.

2 Heat the olive oil in a roasting tin on the hob and then lay the sea bass in the tin. Fry for a couple of minutes until one side of the fish is slightly browned. Carefully lift the fish by its gills, turn it over and caramelise the other side.

3 Transfer the fish to the oven and roast for 12–15 minutes.

4 While the bass is in the oven, finely slice the mushrooms and fry them for a couple of minutes in butter.

5 Serve from the roasting tin, garnishing the fish with the mushrooms and parsley. Mix the buttery juices from the mushroom pan with the juices from the roasting tin and pour this flavoursome mixture over the fish. Unbeatable.

Sea bass flavoured with curry, roasted for about 12 minutes and finished with Sauternes and fresh coriander

Serves 2

1 Preheat the oven to 190°C/gas 5.

2 Season both sides of the bass generously with a good dusting of the curry powder. Heat 5–6 tablespoons of olive oil in a roasting tin on the hob and then lay the sea bass in the tin so that the fish begins to turn golden. Holding the fish by its gills, turn it and begin to brown the other side.

3 Arrange the bay leaves, thyme, star anise and coriander seeds on top of the bass, and sprinkle a pinch of curry powder into the oil around the fish. Continue to cook on the hob for a minute so that both sides have browned a bit. Transfer the fish to the oven to roast for 12 minutes.

4 Meanwhile, in a saucepan, boil the Sauternes until it has evaporated and reduced in volume by about two-thirds; this should take a few minutes.

5 Serve the fish from the roasting tin – garnish with the coriander and pour the syrupy, reduced Sauternes onto the fish at the table.

1 whole sea bass, about 1 kg
A generous amount of mild
  curry powder
Extra virgin olive oil
3 bay leaves
4 sprigs of fresh thyme
3 whole star anise
1 teaspoon coriander seeds,
  crushed
100ml Sauternes (or another
  dessert wine)
Fresh coriander (or fresh
  herbs of your choice),
  to garnish

A whole sea bass with lots of aniseed flavours, cooked en papillote for about 15 minutes

Serves 2

Extra virgin olive oil
1 whole sea bass, about 1kg
¼ small fennel bulb, peeled
   and cut into julienne slices
2 whole star anise
A splash of Pernod (or Ricard)
1 lemon, for squeezing
Maldon sea salt
Fresh tarragon and coriander
   (or fresh herbs of your
   choice), to garnish

1 Preheat the oven to 190°C/gas 5.
2 Lay a piece of foil that is at least twice the size the fish on the work surface. Pour about a teaspoon of olive oil into the centre of the foil and rub it around – just enough to stop the fish sticking to the foil.
3 Lay the sea bass onto the centre of the foil and arrange the fennel and star anise on top of the fish. Add the splash of Pernod.
4 Fold the foil and scrunch the edges of the foil to seal, so that the flavours will be captured within. It should be half-moon shaped.
5 Put the foiled fish in a roasting tin and then place it on the hob and cook over a medium heat for a couple of minutes. Transfer the tin straight to the oven and bake for 15 minutes. The foil will puff up and look like a large silver Cornish pasty, or rather, it *should*.
6 Remove the foiled fish from the oven and carefully open the foil at the table. Add a splash of olive oil, a squeeze of lemon, a sprinkling of sea salt, tarragon and coriander.

A whole sea bass with spring onions, ginger, fresh coriander, cooked en papillote for about 15 minutes

Serves 2

1 sea bass, about 1kg
Extra virgin olive oil
1 dessertspoon white wine
1 piece of fresh ginger,
  peeled and finely sliced
  into matchsticks
2 spring onions, finely
  sliced lengthways
Fresh coriander leaves
  (or fresh herbs of your
  choice), to garnish

1 Preheat the oven to 190°C/gas 5.

2 Lay a piece of foil that is large enough to fold over the fish on the work surface. Pour a teaspoon of olive oil into the centre of the foil and rub it around, just enough to stop the fish sticking to the foil during cooking.

3 Lay the sea bass into the centre of the foil and pour over the wine. Fold the foil, and scrunch around the edges so that all the flavours will be captured within. It should now be shaped like a half-moon.

4 Carefully place the foiled fish in a roasting tin and cook over a medium heat on the hob for a couple of minutes. Transfer the tin straight to the oven and bake for 15–17 minutes.

5 Meanwhile, blanch the ginger. As soon as the water boils, drain the ginger, pouring the hot water momentarily over the spring onions, just enough to soften them. Refresh the ginger by holding it under cold water for a few seconds.

6 Remove the foiled fish from the oven and carefully open the foil at the table. Garnish with the ginger, spring onions and coriander before serving.

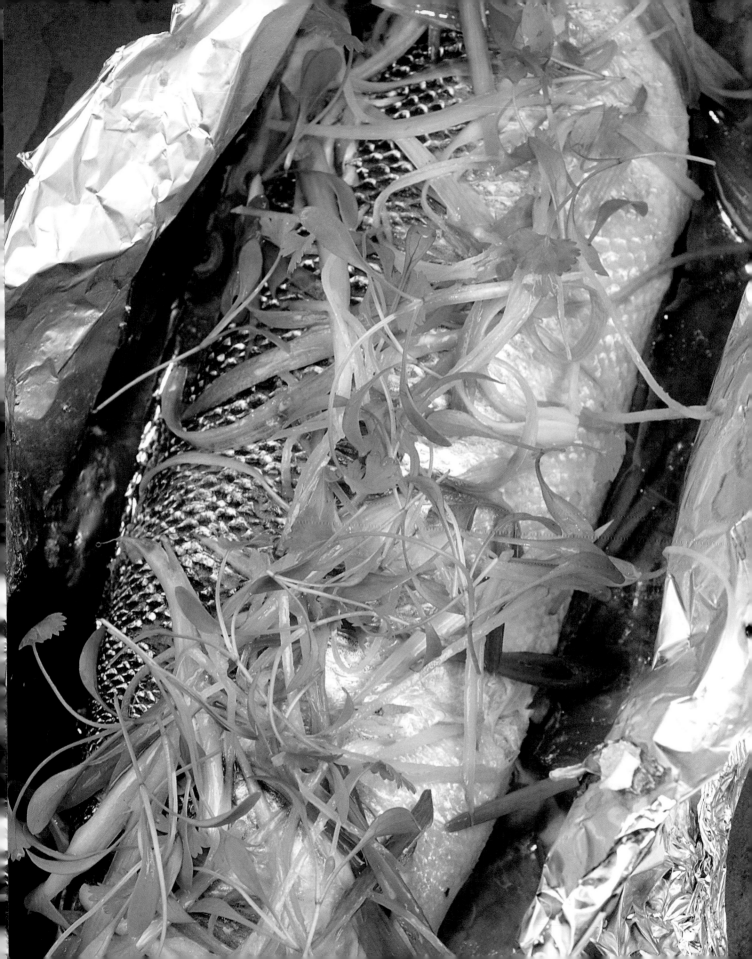

Whole seabream, Oriental-style

Serves 2

1 piece fresh ginger,
  cut lengthways into
  matchsticks
Lemon juice
2 spring onions, cut
  lengthways
1 whole sea bream,
  about 600g
Extra virgin olive oil
Fresh coriander (or fresh
  herbs of your choice),
  to garnish

For the dressing
2 dessertspoons
  toasted sesame oil
2 dessertspoons light
  soy sauce
1 red chilli, deseeded
  and finely sliced

1 Preheat the oven to 190°C/gas 5.
2 Put the ginger and lemon juice into a small
saucepan and cover with a splash of water. Bring to
the boil, wait 20 seconds and then remove from the
heat. As soon as the water boils, drain the ginger,
pouring the hot water momentarily over the spring
onions, just enough to soften them. Refresh the ginger
by holding it under cold water for a few seconds.
3 In a roasting tin on the hob, heat the olive oil and
then brown the fish on one side. Turn it, brown the
other side and transfer the tin to the oven to roast
for 10–12 minutes. While the fish roasts, combine
the sesame oil, soy sauce, and chilli.
4 Serve the fish with the ginger and spring onions
scattered over, then pour over the soy-oil mixture
and sprinkle with coriander.

Red mullet with a sauce of tomato juice and cumin

Serves 2

1 In a large frying pan, shallow-fry the red mullet in some olive oil for about 3 minutes on each side, or longer depending on the size of the fish, until golden.
2 Meanwhile, make the sauce in another pan by bringing to the boil the tomato juice, 1 teaspoon of olive oil and the cumin. Add the butter and stir once. If using celery leaves, shallow fry them in olive oil.
3 Spoon the tomato sauce onto a plate, lay the fish on top of the sauce. Garnish with the celery leaves and serve. Healthy and packed with flavour.

2 whole red mullet,
   about 100g each
Extra virgin olive oil
100ml tomato juice
A pinch of ground cumin
A knob of unsalted butter
A handful of celery
   leaves, to garnish

Four more ways with red mullet

Serves 2

2 red mullet, about 100g each
Extra virgin olive oil
A handful of fresh herbs, to garnish

Cook the pair of mullet like this: in a pan, shallow fry them in olive oil over a medium heat for 3-4 minutes on each side (depending on the size of the fish).

with pesto and a few capers

Top left

1 tablespoon pesto
1 teaspoon capers
Maldon sea salt

1 Mix the pesto with two tablespoons of olive oil and add the capers. Set aside until you are ready to cook the fish.
2 Fry the mullet as described above.
3 Remove the fish from the pan and season it with a few crystals of sea salt. Spoon over the pesto-caper sauce; scatter the herbs (torn basil leaves work well here) and serve.

with porcini and a Madeira reduction

Bottom left

50ml Madeira
1 tablespoon truffle oil
1-2 teaspoons Porcini powder
A handful or two of dried porcini

1 In a small saucepan, boil the Madeira until it has evaporated, thickened and reduced in volume to about a dessertspoon. Pour this syrup into a bowl and combine it with the truffle oil.
2 Season the red mullet with a coating of porcini powder. Cook the mullet as described above.
3 Assemble on the plate: first the red mullet, then sprinkle salt. Scatter fresh parsley.

Oriental-style

Top right

2 whole star anise,
1 piece of fresh ginger, unpeeled and sliced to the size of matchsticks
1 large spring onion, finely sliced lengthways

1 Blanch the ginger matchsticks by putting them in a saucepan of water and bringing to the boil. When the water boils count to 10, remove the pan from the heat and drain through a colander, pouring the hot water momentarily over the spring onions, just enough to soften them.
2 Fry the mullet as described at the top of this page.
3 Serve with the star anise, ginger spring onions spooned on and around the fish, and add the herbs.

with tapenade and fresh basil

Bottom right

1 heaped tablespoon tapenade
A handful of basil leaves

1 Thin the tapenade by mixing it with 3 tablespoons of olive oil.
2 Fry the red mullet as described at the top of this page.
3 Serve the fish with the thinned tapenade spooned onto it, and the basil leaves dropped on and around the mullet. then sprinkle salt. Scatter with fresh herbs (finely chopped parsley works well).

I'm giving you lots of steak dishes here because we all love steak. Prefer rump or rib-eye? Then use rump or rib-eye. The roasted calf's liver is very special and again, the double pork chop dishes require only a few ingredients because that pork has to be the star of the show. The more you add the more you take away…

Meat

★ ★ ★

Peppered steak

Serves 4

4 fillet steaks, about
   180g each
Cracked black pepper
3 tablespoons extra
   virgin olive oil
100ml Lea & Perrins
   Worcestershire sauce
150ml double cream

1 Dust one side of each steak with the pepper so that the pepper sticks to the surface of the meat.
2 In a heavy-based frying pan, heat the olive oil and fry the steaks, pepper-side up, for 3–4 minutes. Turn the steaks and continue to fry for a further 3–4 minutes.
3 Remove the pan from the heat and allow the steaks to rest in the pan in a warm part of the kitchen for 5–10 minutes. Remove the steaks from the pan and put to one side. The juices that are left in the frying pan are delicious, so don't discard them.
4 Meanwhile, make the sauce. First, pour the Worcestershire sauce into the same pan and heat, but don't bring to the boil. Cook until the sauce has reduced by about two-thirds. Now add the cream, keep it on the heat and stir. That's your sauce done.
5 Return the steaks to the hot sauce in the pan and serve.

Fillet steak with peppercorn sauce

Serves 2

1 In a saucepan, bring the Worcestershire sauce to the boil and cook for a few minutes until it reduces in volume by about two-thirds. Remove the pan from the heat and pour in the cream. Add the green peppercorns and the pinch of stock cube. Taste it – nice?

2 In a heavy-based frying pan or sauté pan, heat the olive oil and fry the steaks for 3–4 minutes on each side, turning them only once. Remove the pan from the heat and allow the steaks to rest in a warm part of the kitchen for 5–10 minutes.

3 Put the steaks in the pan of very nice peppercorn sauce and serve.

100ml Lea & Perrins Worcestershire sauce
100ml double cream
1 teaspoon green peppercorns
A pinch of 1 Knorr chicken stock cube
1 tablespoon extra virgin olive oil
2 fillet steaks, about 180g each

Roast rump of lamb with clams and roasting juices

Serves 2–3

1 tablespoon extra virgin
  olive oil (or clarified butter)
Rump of lamb, about 350g
A splash of white wine
2 bay leaves, to garnish
1 sprig of fresh thyme,
  to garnish
About 150g clams

1 Preheat the oven to 180°C/gas 4.
2 Heat olive oil or butter in a non-stick frying pan
and caramelise the lamb on both sides. Transfer
the lamb to a roasting tin, skin-side down, place
in the oven and roast for 10–15 minutes.
3 Remove the lamb from the oven and allow the
meat to rest for 5–10 minutes, but don't discard
the roasting juices.
4 Heat a saucepan and pour in the white wine, bay
leaves and thyme. Add the clams to the pan, cover
with a lid and let them steam for a minute. Lift the
lid, splash olive oil over the clams, cover again and
shake the pan. Discard any clams that do not open.
5 Pour the roasting juices over the lamb, add the
clams and garnish the meat with the thyme and
bay leaves.

Roast rump of lamb with wild mushrooms and roasting juices

Serves 2–3

1 Preheat the oven to 180°C/gas 4.

2 Heat the olive oil or butter in a non-stick frying pan and caramelise the lamb on both sides. Transfer the lamb to a roasting tin, skin-side down, place in the oven and roast for 10–15 minutes.

3 Remove the lamb from the oven and allow the meat to rest for 5–10 minutes, but don't discard the roasting juices.

4 Meanwhile, boil the Madeira in a saucepan until it has evaporated and reduced to almost a syrup. Combine the roasting juices with the Madeira reduction.

5 In a pan, fry the mushrooms in olive oil over a medium heat for a minute or until they are cooked to your taste.

6 To serve, slice the lamb and spoon the mushrooms over and around the meat. Pour over the syrupy juices and scatter with fresh herbs.

Extra virgin olive oil (or clarified butter)
Rump of lamb, about 350g
100ml Madeira
150g wild mushrooms
Fresh herbs of your choice, to garnish

Roast rump of lamb with mint vinaigrette and roasting juices

Serves 2–3

Extra virgin olive oil
(or clarified butter)
Rump of lamb, about 350g
2 teaspoons white wine
vinegar
10g caster sugar
6 fresh mint leaves,
finely chopped
2 shallots, diced, to serve
Fresh herbs of your
choice, to garnish

1 Preheat the oven to 180°C/gas 4.

2 Heat olive oil or butter in a pan and caramelise the lamb on both sides. Transfer the lamb to a roasting tin, skin-side down, place in the oven and roast for 10–15 minutes.

3 Remove the lamb from the oven and allow the meat to rest for 5–10 minutes, but don't discard the roasting juices.

4 In a saucepan, combine the vinegar and sugar and bring to the boil. Add the roasting juices and the chopped mint leaves and continue to heat for a minute or two, so that the flavours meet and mix well.

5 Slice the lamb and pour over the vinaigrette and serve it with a sprinkling of diced shallots and fresh herbs.

Double pork chops roasted with Dijon mustard, dill cucumber and chives

Serves 2

1 double pork chop (2 chops joined, ask your butcher to remove the chine bone and skin, but to leave a layer of fat)
Clarified butter (or extra virgin olive oil)
1 small, sweet dill cucumber
Dijon mustard, to your taste
Fresh chives, finely snipped
Fresh flat-leaf parsley leaves (or fresh herbs of your choice), to garnish

1 Preheat the oven to 160°C/gas 2–3.
2 First brown the chops, skin-side down, for a few minutes in a hot pan of butter. Transfer the chops to an ovenproof dish and roast for 30–40 minutes. Remove the chops from the oven and let the meat rest for 10 minutes in a warm part of the kitchen.
3 Meanwhile, finely slice the dill cucumber, lengthways, then cut into dice.
4 Cover the pork with Dijon mustard and then coat it with the diced dill and chives; they will stick to the mustard. Garnish with parsley before serving.

Double pork chops roasted with prunes and bacon

Serves 2

1 double pork chop (2 chops joined; ask your butcher to remove the chine bone and skin, but to leave a layer of fat)

Clarified butter (or extra virgin olive oil)

100ml port

100ml prune juice

1 dessertspoon double cream

1 teaspoon Knorr concentrated chicken stock

About 50g bacon lardons

6 prunes

1 Preheat the oven to 160°C/gas 2–3.

2 First brown the chops, skin-side down for a few minutes in a hot pan of butter. Transfer the chops to an ovenproof dish and roast for 30–40 minutes. Remove the chops from the oven and let the meat rest for 10 minutes in a warm part of the kitchen.

3 Meanwhile, in a saucepan, boil the port until it has thickened, evaporated and reduced right down to about a teaspoon of syrup. Add the prune juice, cream and chicken stock. Continue to boil for a few minutes, until the sauce has reduced by about half (or to a consistency to your taste).

4 In a separate pan, fry the bacon and prunes in the remaining butter. Take a spoonful of the fat from the lardons and add it to the sauce.

5 Carve the double chops into two, pour over the sauce and garnish with the prunes and bacon.

Double pork chops roasted with morels, Madeira and cream

Serves 2

1 Preheat the oven to 160°C/gas 2–3.

2 First brown the chops, skin-side down for a few minutes in a hot pan of butter. Transfer the chops to an ovenproof dish and roast for 30–40 minutes. Remove the chops from the oven and let the meat rest for 10 minutes in a warm part of the kitchen.

3 Meanwhile, in a saucepan, rapidly boil the Madeira until it is reduced in volume to about a teaspoon of syrup. Stir in the cream and chicken stock, and taste. Reduce to a low heat to keep the sauce warm.

4 In another pan, fry the morels in butter for 2 minutes before draining them in a colander to remove any excess butter. Return them to the pan and combine with the Madeira sauce before serving with the chops. Scatter with fresh herbs.

1 double pork chop (2 chops joined; ask your butcher to remove the chine bone and skin, but to leave a layer of fat)
Clarified butter (or extra virgin olive oil)
100ml Madeira
50ml double cream
1 teaspoon Knorr concentrated chicken stock
100g morels
A knob of unsalted butter
Fresh herbs of your choice, to garnish

Double pork chops roasted with apples and a Marco Polo glaze

Serves 2

1 double pork chop (2 chops
    joined, ask your butcher
    to remove the chine bone
    and skin, but to leave a
    layer of fat)
Clarified butter (or extra
    virgin olive oil)
50ml honey
1 teaspoon coriander seeds
2 whole star anise
10ml water
Fresh herbs of your choice,
    to garnish

1 Preheat the oven to 160°C/gas 2–3.

2 First brown the chops, skin-side down, for a few minutes in a hot pan of melted butter. Transfer the chops to an ovenproof dish and roast for 30–40 minutes. Remove the chops from the oven and let the meat rest for 10 minutes in a warm part of the kitchen.

3 To make the glaze, in a saucepan combine the honey, coriander seeds and star anise with the water in a saucepan. Bring to the boil and cook until it has thickened to your taste. Remove from the heat and stir in the juices from the ovenproof dish.

4 Slice the chop in two. Serve with a star anise on each chop and glaze before serving. Scatter with fresh herbs.

A joint of calf's liver, coated in black pepper, roasted in the oven for about 15 minutes, and served with raisins flamed in Armagnac

Serves 6

About 800g calf's liver
(or whole liver)
Enough finely crushed
black peppercorns to
coat the liver
Clarified butter (or ghee
or extra virgin olive oil)
A handful of raisins or
currants
A generous splash of
Armagnac
Fresh herbs of your choice,
to garnish

1 Preheat the oven to 190°C/gas 5.
2 Dust one side of the liver with the pepper. In a large frying pan, heat the butter and fry the liver, pepper-side down, for 2 minutes. Turn the liver over, so it is now pepper-side up, and transfer it to an ovenproof dish to roast for 12–15 minutes. Remove from the oven and leave to rest in a warm place in the kitchen for a good 10 minutes.
3 Meanwhile, fry the raisins in butter for a minute or so and then pour in a generous splash of Armagnac. It will flame – be careful not to singe your hair.
4 Slice the liver and spoon the raisins, along with their Armagnac-infused butter, over the liver and serve scattered with fresh herbs.

Roasted joint of calf's liver with Dijon mustard and chives

Serves 6

1 Preheat the oven to 190°C/gas 5.
2 In a large frying pan, heat the butter and fry the liver for a couple of minutes, then turn the liver and transfer it to an ovenproof dish to roast for 12–15 minutes. Remove from the oven and leave to rest in a warm place in the kitchen for a good 10 minutes.
3 When the liver is cool enough to handle, spread the mustard over and then roll it in the chives (they'll stick to the mustard). Serve with fresh herbs.

By the way... You could do the same with lamb's liver, again starting it off in the pan before roasting it for about 5 to 8 minutes in the oven.

About 800g calf's liver
(or whole liver)
Clarified butter (or ghee
or extra virgin olive oil)
Dijon mustard, to your taste
2 handfuls of chives, finely
diced
Fresh herbs of your choice,
to garnish

Liver and onions

Serves 1

1 onion, halved and
  finely sliced
A generous amount of
  clarified butter (or
  unsalted butter or ghee)
1 piece of liver
Fresh herbs of your choice,
  to garnish

1 Fry the onion in a generous amount of foaming butter for about 5 minutes, or until it is golden and crisp (but don't burn it). Drain the onion but keep the butter.

2 Fry the liver in the butter. Top the liver with the onions and a scattering of fresh herbs.

Roast chicken with Merlot vinegar

Serves 4

1 chicken, about 1.2kg
5 tablespoons extra virgin
   olive oil
100ml Merlot vinegar
1 shallot, finely chopped
Fresh herbs of your choice,
   to garnish

1 Preheat the oven to 180°C/gas 4.
2 Put the chicken in a large roasting tin and pour over the olive oil. You want the oil to coat the skin of the bird.
3 Roast the chicken in the oven for about 40–50 minutes, basting it a couple of times during cooking, until the chicken is tender.
4 When cooked, remove the chicken from the roasting tin and leave until it is cool to the touch. Reserve all the juices and olive oil that remain in the roasting tin.
5 Boil the vinegar in a frying pan until it has evaporated and reduced in volume by about half. Keep tasting: it will sweeten, thicken and become softer on the palate – and then it will be syrupy.
6 To make the sauce, combine the cooled juices and oil from the roasting tin with the reduced vinegar in the frying pan – give it just a gentle stir so that the liquids are not fully mixed. Carve the chicken, scatter over the chopped shallot and pour over the sauce and add a sprinkling of fresh herbs.

By the way… Often you will be advised to check that roast chicken is cooked by inserting a skewer into the thickest part of the meat to see if the juices run clear. However, when the bird is resting it will continue to cook (albeit at a lower temperature) so take that into consideration – in other words, don't overcook it. If you don't have Merlot vinegar to hand, then why not try a different vinegar; white wine vinegar works well.

Rhubarb burnt cream

Serves 6

400g rhubarb
150g caster sugar
1 tablespoon water

For the burnt cream mix
900ml double cream
100ml whole milk
2 vanilla pods, halved
   and sliced lengthways
9 egg yolks
150g caster sugar, plus
   extra for topping

1 Preheat the oven to 170°C/gas 3.
2 Finely slice the rhubarb and then put in an ovenproof dish with the sugar and mix together. Add the water and cook in the oven for 20 minutes, until the rhubarb has softened.
3 Remove from the oven and drain away the liquid. Using a stick blender, turn the sugary cooked rhubarb into a purée. Now put the purée back into the ovenproof dish (the brulée mix will be poured over it). Reduce the oven temperature to 95°C/gas ¼ .
4 In a separate saucepan combine the cream, milk and vanilla pods and bring to the boil. Meanwhile, in a bowl, whisk together the egg yolks and sugar for a few seconds so they are fully mixed.
5 Pour the boiling cream-milk mixture over the eggs and continue to whisk so that you don't end up with scrambled eggs. Remove the vanilla pods and scrape the seeds into the mixture.
6 Pour the mixture into the ovenproof dish and cook in the oven for 35 minutes.
7 When cooked, remove the dish from the oven and allow to cool. Sprinkle half the sugar over the cream and brown the sugar and make it crunchy, preferably with a kitchen blowtorch, or failing that, by putting it under a hot grill.
8 Leave the caramel topping to cool and then sprinkle over the remaining sugar and repeat the browning process. It should be served immediately.

Cherries Jubilee

Serves 6

1kg cherries
100ml Kirsch
400ml water
250g caster sugar
Ice cream, to serve

1 Slice the cherries or remove the stones and leave whole – your choice.
2 In a saucepan, combine the Kirsch, water and sugar and bring to the boil to make a syrup. Pour the syrup over the cherries and serve immediately with ice cream.

By the way… This dish was created by Escoffier and traditionally the syrup was thickened with cornflour, but I prefer to keep it light, so leave out the flour.

Affogato

Serves 1

1½ dessertspoons Camp
    coffee (or to your taste)
240ml water
2–3 balls of vanilla ice cream

1 Mix the Camp coffee with the water and bring to the boil in a small saucepan.
2 Pour the boiling coffee over the ice cream. Affogato is Italian for drowned – so be generous when you pour.
3 Eat it immediately, while also considering that traditionally you'd need an expensive espresso machine to make this dish.

First published in Great Britain in 2010
by Weidenfeld & Nicolson

1 3 5 7 9 10 8 6 4 2

A CIP catalogue record for this book is available from the British Library.

ISBN: 978 0 297 85651 1

Designed by Smith & Gilmour
Printed and bound in Italy

The Orion Publishing Group's policy is to use papers that are natural,
renewable and recyclable and made from wood grown in sustainable
forests. The logging and manufacturing processes are expected to
conform to environmental regulations of the country of origin.

Weidenfeld & Nicolson

Orion Publishing Group Ltd
Orion House
5 Upper Saint Martin's Lane
London, WC2H 9EA

An Hachette UK Company

www.orionbooks.co.uk